Dwellers

Megan Mary Moore

Dwellers

Megan Mary Moore

Attention schools and businesses: for discounted copies on large
orders, please contact the publisher directly.

For information contact:
Unsolicited Press
Portland, Oregon
www.unsolicitedpress.com
orders@unsolicitedpress.com
619-354-8005

Cover Design: Kathryn Gerhardt
Editor: S.R. Stewart

ISBN: 978-1-950730-21-6

Poems

A woman who utters such depressing and disgusting sounds has no right to be anywhere – no right to live.

— George Bernard Shaw, Pygmalion

Meggie Mae

was born from a storm to a place
where rain stripped wallpaper
and floors stained
when popsicles dripped,
sun made freckles and
chickens made friends,
friends made food

and Meggie Mae, Meggie made
a horrible daughter.

A Trailer is a Tower Who Got Tired

Needed a rest, a lay down on his side.
Why didn't he get back up? He loved watching us.
Me in my too-big pants and too big words
Mom's cigarette fingernails, Dad's asbestos tongue.
He didn't get back up because
because
he loved me.

1 a.m. Listening to the Neighbors

Catch a break, catch the flu.
No witnesses   no crime.
Seven years old: lips were bologna
and kisses made sandwiches
and I trapped caterpillars when
no one knew. They were asleep and
I had greedy hands, scooping
up bugs and listening.
No crime   no witnesses.

Heard and swore he said,
Here's a gun. You don't deserve to live.
No way Jose. No gun in this home.
A careful tongue   a careless ear:
Here's a cunt who don't deserve to live.

In the light I pulled out my captive caterpillars,
Big, deep breaths as they crawled through my fingers
I'd love them still as I loved them then
before I knew they were maggots.

Dwellers

Because we didn't own, Aunt Crystal called us
Dwellers. People who borrowed place,
rented memory, ready to run.
We didn't plant flowers
because we'd leave them behind. We
dwelt among the dandelions instead.
Weeds upon weeds upon weeds.

Mothers and Daughters

Whispers from mothers
turn to spells from daughters:
Don't throw out the
baby with the water,
three hours later and
she is pigtailed, pink mouthed:
Throw out the baby,
don't waste the water.

Babies have babies,
and mothers
hush
hush
hush
until all of the water,
and all of the babies
are flushed.

It's Ok to Hate Your Sister In Aurora, IN

In the creek, in the crik,
my stone sinks, her stone skips.

Aurora, a grunt in her throat,
a grunt in our home.

Christmas creaks
and Christ calls us, home

is how to fold a fitted sheet.
Gift of bicycle bells

in the Bible Belt
lulled me to sleep.

Momma dropped
me on my head

when she saw the yellow smiley
on the bathroom door.

How much paint did it take?
For mother's other daughter

to make the potty smile?
The next family will take paint,

$200 in paint, to the hide

the smile Sissy made.

In Case of Fire

Momma carried me with the able-bodied
ladies who carried their wheelchair-bound men.
Two shirtless guys ran in front of us down
the stairs, each with a snake
around his neck. Red welts grew
on my cheeks, usually from
penicillin, ibuprofen, amoxicillin,
but this time from fire

chasing us.
2 a.m. blackberry night,
I saw flames and snakes' eyes
warning me: *It's like this in hell,*
it's like this when you die.
Momma set me down, and I ran
in urine-soaked socks
away from home.

Goddamn Meggie

followed him to the river
jumped in after the bag
to rescue the goddamn-
God damn the kittens
not you, Meggie. Meggie, ain't
not your job to rescue nothin.

Then who? *God, damnit.*

God gives and gives and gives
even when he takes he gives.
God gives safety and the end,
safety in the end.
God gives
the end.

American Girls

Kimberly was my aunt's
before she was mine.
I rescued her from cedar chest,
smuggled her home.
Mothball smell stung her plastic hair
and I tugged at her bleach blonde
tangles until handfuls came out.
She roller-skated, bald
past the other dolls,
painted to look like
the girls who groomed them.

In the mirror I confessed my love
for her blue glare and squeaky
hip flexors. The other dolls
were scared of her
when she spun to face them
under my hands.
I was, too.

Cardboard Coffin

Momma entered me in coloring contests
across the tristate. I won every time.

One prize was a Meggie sized coffin
filled with candy,

cardboard, spray painted black.
I dug through and climbed inside.

Among Whoppers and Smarties.
I held the certificate to the light,

my name: Megan Mary
my address: 156 Sandusky

my age: 4.
Wrong. 6.

Momma, you put the wrong age.
Momma musta made a mistake.

No, baby, only way you'll win.
You enjoy your coffin.

Sarah Had a

Pink Barbie Raincoat
slick shine stick to itself
peel it from her cubby
I watched her in it.
button buttons up to chin
and then run through puddles.

I had a red poncho
greatgramma made
years years years ago,
but now it was mine
threadbare but BRIGHT
red,holding me

Mrs. Something pulled me
from recess called Momma, said
the poncho wasn't enough
said I'd have to sit in
said maybe buy me a
Pink Barbie Raincoatlike Sarah had.

Sisters

Between Sissy and me
were four dead babies.
But Sissy said one lived,
said momma built a wall around her
a sliver of space big enough
for little girls to stay little
and bad girls to get badder.
and if you thump loud enough,
you can hear her moan.
Agatha.

She ate the dirt and her own hair.
She cried when it rained, she hated water.
I knew she was there, my blood
would go cold when she was mad,
blood we shared.

What had she done
that we hadn't done
to get locked away?
I didn't ask her, afraid
of the answer.

Home Water

Muddy river rumbles through Kentucky,
doesn't swish slosh swish like the ocean
but rumbles over boulders and flings
fish downstream. Ugly, muddy, green,
the only body of water I ever seen.
The only body I ever seen.

Sandusky

There have been so many dead
cats but few dead
men   in the places I've lived.

They hid his body in their storage unit.
Mom and Dad ran the office
and we lived there. I walked up and through,
- can't go under it, can't go over it –
and I smelled him.
More than garbage can,
garbage cats, garbage men,
dead men smell more.

They thought I hated home
because the dead
man was found. Out my window
the boxes and boxes
of other people's maybe laters,
I missed him.
Dead Man smell gone
and me, alone.

Mom and Dad had a blood money trail
it takes money to hide a body.
Bloody body money, but they didn't know.
Grocery bag crinkle through sweaty
bills. Blood bills. They were sorry.
We were poorer.

Polaroid of an Albino Deer

The albino deer ate honeysuckle
wherever honeysuckle was.
We watched her, everyone,
took Polaroids and shook.
Somebody put a salt lick,
illegal, on our hill
to get her to stay
a little longer.
But she was smarter,
a blur that left us always shaking,
waiting for the next time she'd slip,
we'd click and whisper.
Our landlord groaned:
The bitch is off again.

What Kenny Carried

Kenny carried his keys in his mouth because
he was hit in the head. Somebody hit him
hard and took his money. After that,
he held his hands to his chest like a t-rex.
Mom said he didn't have a job,
still he climbed in his car every day,
keys in teeth, and waved goodbye to me.
But he didn't leave.

I was making dandelion chains
when he grabbed me,
pushed me into his apartment, jingling always.
Help me, through his teeth.   *Ok.*
And in his living room:
the albino deer on her side,
blinking, breathing, drowning,
big and barely alive.
She hurt he said and
dropped his keys.

He had carried her inside. He must
have been strong, his t-rex arms.
Can I touch her? because
Kenny was grown up and I was not.
Touch her, just an echo,
but I did. She was not soft.
Together we watched her die.
Eyes don't close when you die.

The Loch Ness Monster Was Found Dead in Kentucky

beached on the river bank. How did she make it to
        Kentucky
without being noticed? *Carefully,* said the newscaster.
She was wearing MAC and carrying Chanel.
Nessie was a hell of a gal said some fucking merman.
I think she had family there said the same fucking merman
when asked why Kentucky.

Her grandparents had been rag people along the Ohio.
A wagon of rags, yelling *RAGS FOR SALE* for hours
a day. And Nessie, she didn't want to be the Rag Monster,
she left and learned that less pays more. She made her
appearances few, always keeping her name in mouths.
When she knew it was time, she left Loch Ness, for home.

The Drowned

Awake before my parents,
I saw a man fall
from a telephone pole
from my balcony window
and another man
among the wires
screamed for me to help,
for anyone to help.
I thought his friend
wearing a lifejacket
on the ground had drowned.

It wasn't a lifejacket,
the orange vest
that workers wore
in the sky while
working on the sunrise.
I had never been to the ocean,
but I'd seen it on TV.
Maybe there was one
behind the woods,
past the poison ivy.

Now when I picture the ocean
the dead man
is smiling in orange,
afloat in the crashing foam,
bobbing in blue,

stolen from Ohio,
carried through the air
to the ocean
where he belongs.

In a Past Life

I was a magpie.
Each feather fell easy from the
skin I was born in.
I wait in the breath
between skin and
curling iron, burning
off my hair
to be the bird
I was
again.

God's favorite bird.
God's favorite girl.

I Take Care

of grandma's splintered nailbeds
of grandma's sagging skin
pricked, pierced, pinned

by the bed of nails she lives in.
It's my job to clean her accidents
because I don't gag.

She didn't clean mine as a baby,
she didn't love me.
Didn't love any baby.

I ask my mother, do you remember her kissing,
hugging? *No, no one. No, never.*
Grandma believes I'm killing her

and begs our family
to save her from me. And I beg
for the same.

We wait together
for nightgowns to tangle
to strangle   the stars goodnight.

Postoperative Psychosis

When she wakes up, she yells that the man in the scrubs has a
      tattoo
of a bird on his stomach. The symbol of the people who want her
      dead.

She tells me before my mother was born she and grandpa were
      spies.
When he died, her cover was blown. And now the doctors know.

I get her to stop screaming by taking the clock from the wall
and waving it out the window. A sign to her allies it's time.

Her years as a spy made her rough and
afraid to love. It wasn't that she didn't love us.

Back in her body, her first words were
I hoped I wouldn't see you again.

We don't tell her about her life as a spy.

I Remember Praying to Princesses

and slapping myself to sleep
because we knew,
me and God,
where I belonged.
Perpetual stepsister:
eyes pecked, toes sawed.

I don't want to think about it,
but it plays with me, the men in charge
and the things they'd say while they watch me
cut each piggy to try and fit:
Cow and her bleedin hoof,
another chick to die.

How to Dance

I've never seen
moonlight and waterlilies
dance but some say they can.
I tell this to Emily as she works
on her taxidermy. She's stuffing a mouse
she found by the dumpster.
She dresses him in a hat meant for Ken
and tells me: *He's the one
who teaches them to dance.*

Girls Bathroom

We kiss ourselves
in the mirror,
to leave our
print kisses.
Bomb berry deep
and peony petal pink,
2 lips, 4 lips
left on our reflection.

Linda Sue, the cleaning lady, scrubs
our kisses after we've gone.
4 lips, 2 kisses gone,
but not soon enough.
Girls piss, puddle
drip, slip
and they see
our kiss.

Blue Doesn't Occur in Nature

I understand this New Years Eve, 2008.
I want lights, black magic,
blinking neon glitter bombs.
God was willing to give
       green.

He closed the banks and threw us the sun
but bit, swallowed, and chewed blue
to keep in his belly forever.

I dream that I'll find it
bubbling up from a lullaby.
Blue: the color spit down to us from
the man in the moon.

Trailer Trash

He killed cats,
sold them to the butcher,
never said what then,
butch, he guessed, the cats.
Walked home with nickels in mouth.
Mine too, mouth too, metal mouth, kissed then.

Can't you just kill chickens?
No   mo   ney.
Dropped the chocolate bar
in the soapy water,
teeth shave suds and spit nickels.
Thank you, kitty. For your sacrifice.

Accelerated Readers

Because we were the smartest kids
in school, we were supposed to date.
They still have a picture of us framed
in the hall, next to a plaque that says
"Most Accelerated Readers."

He got out of jail two months ago
and asked my fiancé
if he wanted anything
he was growing. He did,
we visited him.

You was the first girl I hugged.
he laughs and shoves
a pit bull away from the
bag of brownies he hands to us.
We hug again.

At the Craft Fair

the woman dunks the stuffed bunnies in hot wax
submerges their stitched mouths, noses,
and every tuft of fluff that was once soft to touch.
And when the thing comes up, it could prick a man each
hair now heavy with the candle crust.

I reach out to touch and she slaps my hand.
They aren't toys anymore.
Are they candles now?
If it smells, it was meant to burn.

Driving my Cousin Home from Visiting Grandpa in Hospice

You aren't ugly, she says.
Thank you.
Mom said you were the ugly sheep of the family.
You mean the black sheep.
No. Ugly.

She flicks the crucifix hung on the rearview mirror by my mother.

Hello. Enclosed are the Remains of Your Loved One.
The University of Cincinnati Thanks You.

Grandpa came back to us in the mail
after the university used his body

for whatever science they use 90-year-old bodies for.
My aunt spit on me when I told her that

he had asked for his ashes
to be buried in the backyard under the concrete frog.

She didn't say she didn't believe
that he'd said it, didn't say I was wrong.

She wasn't invited when grandma, mom, and I buried him
under the frog, next to Stevie Lee, the fish who lived

for five years. Mom dug a little grave for grandpa
the way she did for Stevie Lee, the Golden Wonder.

I Asked My Dad if He Was Happy When I Was Born

I prayed you wouldn't end up a girl.
His appendix broke when I slid out. If I had been a son
I could have been the sun, glittering and great,
demanding respect for my catastrophic weight.

Aphrodite came from foam, but me -I from a rib.
Like Eve and Snow White, I was built to devour,
the dough, the clay, the meat

and I will
lick each rib
clean.

These Memories are Mine, Not My Mother's

The smell of leaves in my hair
from recess, from running,
somersaulting through grass and dandelions
(ugly
little
weeds)
and the smell stayed because no hot water
to shower, it didn't matter. Greasy, leaf-y
hair, smudged cheeks.
(ugly
little
me)

Sheet Ghost

He came back as a sheet ghost.
I recognized his wrinkles through the eyeholes.

Leon Redbone played him in.
It took him years to find me,

his blinks told me this.
He laid down in my bed.

His breath pushed at the sheet
like a baby kicking to be born.

Ghosts are warm.
I held the edge of his sheet,

fraying, as old as Earth.
Where do ghosts go?

He answered with his
body, floating, leaving,

up.

Emily Nightmares

falling up my apartment stairs.
The steepest stairs she's ever seen.
Every day after school she braced herself
to follow me   up   up   up
where we'd brownie-breath whisper
about girls in class.

She admits the dreams after I move
but her night falling continues.
I feel bad, like I've pushed her,
until I ask her and hear her answer:
What's at the top? After you fall up?
Poppies.

Love Poem

I claimed the cat who lived
in the dumpster. His tail cut to a stump.
I called him Stubby
and he loved me almost as much
as I loved him. I fed him
bologna and rocked him to sleep.

Dad went outside to smoke. He thought
I was asleep, but I was up, watching him
through my window. And he saw
Stubby's body before I did.
I watched him throw his head back
before scooping up my cat.

He cradled him like a child
before slipping him in the dumpster
through the door on the side.
Reached into his pocket, swallowed
a handful of something before
coming back inside.

Saving Time

She never married babies' daddies because
she had things to kill, and time to save.

She skins deer in her shed
and makes curtains out of them.

She shoots the birds who wake her
from her bedroom window.

She invites ants in the house so she can squish
them before they make it to the kitchen

She braids her hair with fur and feathers,
plants her feet deep in the mud each morning,

warning women who may want to love her.

The Apartments Across from St. Aloysius Gonzaga

Ashley and I cartwheeled hoping the cars would honk and they
        did.

We waved at people filing out the doors until an old lady grabbed
Ashley, said she should be in church not a 2-piece.

We heard a moan from the side where they buried the dead
and Ashley said a ghost had come from hell and dared me to see.

A wrinkled man curled on the grass, moaning and rocking, and
Ashley was right. He looked at me and cried. I knew

I would go to hell when I died.

In 6th Grade

the sun was the most beautiful
thing because it hurt to stare.
At 12 she taught me being beautiful
and falling asleep were the same.

On the floor together.
we thought the boys were for love
and we were for practice.

And I'm sorry we never
said what we thought –
never said we were wrong.
We were wrong.

I Wanted to Leave Home

the way Charlie McCarthy wanted to leave Edgar Bergen.
He didn't say he wanted to be a real boy,
he wanted to use his wooden limbs to hold
an actress to his unhinged jaw,
feel Patron dribble down his chin.

I think about Ed laying him down, saying
Ok, it's yours now, the world.
And Charlie's hollow head hitting the ground,
limbs limp, top hat tumbling away. And Charlie
paralyzed.

My Ceiling Fell in on Me

while I was touching myself.
There are no private times here.
God gapes and pinches
my head between plaster and mattress.
Mattress springs and ceilings fall,
but if He wanted me to stop,
it didn't work. Above me, the sky

opened up, ate me up. In the moon's
big belly I finished, covered in
insulation, sweet, itchy, sick
pink around me, like lying in a field
of cotton candy, starlight burning skin.

Maybe He just wanted to remind me,
Meggie Mae is never alone, never,
we all live together,
under the same
moonstrosity.

Girlhood

Panties around our ankles and Bible in our laps,
we wonder if She knew that girls would cry
to Her, to Her son, to let it come.

Because

when Gabriel came, Mary was surrounded
by glossy magazines, sugary music, like syrup
pouring over Her from a machine in the corner.
A tornado of lip gloss, body sprays
without bottles, circling her head,
and the sticky notion of skin buried in that storm.

And

that was the last of that. Hazy, purple daydreams
no more. Knees will bruise from prayer
-*When Christ comes, may our wombs be spared.*
We wake up to a deep red ink blot
bust of the Virgin with flowing veil,
staining flowered sheets, not
a curse   but a kiss
            from Eve   from Mary.

Roadkill

On the drive back,
the street light floods
the roadkill in
golden dust.
His neck broken,
fur blowing.
I keep driving,
because I need to
be in bed.
There is no one

on the road
so I can drive as slowly
as I am. And I am
driving slowly
because of that animal
dead in the road.

I can still see
in the rearview,
the dead thing
fall up into the light,
limbs limp, gracefully carried
through whatever stardust
chose to fall between the trees,
whatever heaven has to be
for animals in the road.

In the Holy of Holies or the Last Stall in the Basement of St. Elizabeth High School

Pencil fell, door slammed, and I'm safe.
These fingers not writing
about our Heavenly Father,
taking a break.
White blouses reek of
bleach and pollen
against the cardboard stall,
sweat clinging and I'm stuck.
Plaid skirt that's never rolled up,
no   is up   oh.

I saw God there.
Halo of soap bubbles
that I forced under fingernails
and scrub, scrub, scrub.
In a haze of disinfectant
and cistern spit-up:
Come, my child.
God, I did.
To you
to her   to him   to them.

With the steam, He is gone
and I'm left with lip gloss
that whispers: no more
-no, more. Door slams.

I Was Voted Most Likely to Become a Housewife

But I should be in jail for
thought crime after thought crime.

Falling asleep in backyards
in nothing but my apron,

hair crisp from the sizzle of church bells.
Those who hate my apple pie

have never been in love.

Love Poem 2

1989: Dad's ex-wife, Terry,
went on a talk show to talk
about the divorce.
She knew it was wrong
because she loved the dog,
The Fonz, more.
The Fonz was invited
on the show. Dad wasn't.

2009: he calls me at 3 a.m.
begging for Terry.
She died before I was born.
He's working and crying in Indianapolis.

Time moves different in Indianapolis.
It drags you backward until you've died
in every year you were alive.

Where's Terry? Where's Terry? Where's Terry?
I've learned what to say
to let him sleep his way back to 1993.
I killed her, Dad. And The Fonz, too.

I Met the Devil in the Woods

She held my hand
and walked with me.
She said my aunts had warned
me: get closer to God,
reach for more
than I was given, for heaven.
Blame me,

she said. She created
my cavities,
claimed my body
from inside
my mouth.
There was nothing
my aunts could do.

She squeezed
my hand and we walked
slower and I knew
she'd never leave.
They don't love me,
I told her.
Blame me.

It's not all bad.
Her long nails bit
my palm. Between

her lips, a heated hiss:
Boys love the smell
of your dirty hair.

Long Pigs Eat Long Pig

 My aunts taught me that
not with words, but with teeth
And prayer. They hated my dirty hair
and soft body, meaty and sweet,
and my mother who I came from,

who taught me, barefoot, to run
through wildflowers, in dirty white
dresses to show girls and boys we loved
how pretty, how free, while running
away from sisters with teeth.

Loving a Man with a Dead Dad

Alan knocked on a neighbor's door at 2 a.m. and was shot.
No one knows why he knocked but the neighbor got scared so he
     shot.

The man who shot Alan was 72 and could only drag the body to
     the backyard.
He started digging the grave, got tired, and called his friend for
     help.

But not until a week later
after Alan started to rot.

Alan was buried in the cemetery before they built the McDonald's
     across the street,
but we're glad they built it. We get ice cream before we visit.

Ben was 13 when Alan knocked, was shot, started to rot. Now 23,
     his ice cream cone
drips on the marker and tells me a psychic asked to call Alan back.

Ben said no.
We don't knock.

St. Elizabeth Seton Watched Me

pull out in front of a truck.
She stood stone-faced at the crunch
of red metal and pelvic bone.
Sirens like a distant ache
in her sainted skull.

My pelvis quaked in three places,
three fault lines through my bone
forever. Lines so thick that
I can't carry babies in me
without breaking again.

My bone took from
August to August to heal,
one year in bed and every day
Elizabeth sent them after me,
the ghosts of the babies
who would not live in me.
Tiny fingernails dug at my skin
when the sun went down
to remind me I killed them,
not myself.

I walked with a cane after August,
my unborn infants behind.
I visited Elizabeth to show her
I kept her curse close.
The guilt of a dozen
tiny hands and knees

following always.
She kept them at her feet
when I walked away,
all but one who
climbed my hip,
bouncing against my breaks.
He kissed my face.

The Creek on Stoney Hollow Road

I hear the ground drink,
not the water seep. Earth acts.
She wants to swallow me, too.
I let her taste my sweat and bite
at the hair on my arms.

One wild night, the Earth and me
will finish what my parents started.
Until then, I squish-step, wet
away from her creek,
Tease, Earth splashes.

Mary, Mary, Quite Contrary

How does your garden grow? A gift from a God
and it is good, that's all we need to know.
Jesus came to save the sinners from sin
And Mary Magdalene, she said to him
sorry.

Did they love each other? Did they fuck?
He loves everyone. Jesus. Did she get jealous? Mary.
It is his job to love everyone. And it was her job to say
sorry.

If Body Dysmporphia Follows Me To Death

It's proportional to your weight, Charon explains
as he peels the coins from my eyelids.
This would get a girl about half your size across.
He has a yellow rubber rain hat that protects
him from the Styx spit.
He is used to it, I'm not.
No one told me, I say, meaning the price.

No mirrors in Ohio? He asks, meaning my size.
So, I'm stuck? We look at the river together. *Stuck.*
He hops in his boat and I sit shoreside,
look back to the cloud I came from,
dancing fast away from me. And I look
to Charon. He waves, rowing away.
Just doing his job.

Marie Antoinette's Last Words Were

Pardon me, sir, I didn't mean to do that.
She had accidentally stepped on the foot
of the executioner and was apologizing for it.
It must have been something to see her
without her wig, all of France at her feet,
apologizing to the man
who would take her head.

He Donated His Body to Science

Not medical but physics.·
Decomposition in Orbit,
and someone calculated how far he went,
what gravity, speed, time
mattered to a corpse. Not much,
they concluded.
Not much at all.

Acknowledgements

Both "I Asked My Dad if He Was Happy When I Was Born," and "I Was Voted Most Likely to Be a Housewife" were previously published in *Capulet Magazine*. "If My Body Dysmporphia Follows Me to Death" first appeared in *Rattle*. "Sisters" first appeared in *Haunted are These Houses* published by *Unnerving Magazine*. I want to thank these outlets for giving these poems their first home.

And thank you Mom and Dad.

About the Author

Megan Mary Moore is a poet from Cincinnati, Ohio. Moore holds an MFA from Miami University and her poetry has been featured in journals including *Capulet Magazine* and *Moonsick Magazine*.

About the Press

Unsolicited Press is a small press in Portland, Oregon. The progressive publishing house was founded in 2012 by editors who desired a stronger connection with writers. The team publishes award-winning fiction, poetry, and creative nonfiction.

Learn more at www.unsolicitedpress.com.